The Complete Keto Diet Cookbook for Beginners

Simple, Quick & Easy Ketogenic Diet Recipes
That Will Help You Burn Fat Forever

Charlie Stewart

Warning-Disclaimer

The purpose of this book is to educate and entertain. The author or publisher does not guarantee that anyone following the techniques, suggestions, tInstant Pots, ideas, or strategies will become successful. The author and publisher shall have neither liability or responsibility to anyone with respect to any loss or damage caused, or alleged to be caused, directly or indirectly by the information contained in this book.

Contents

Introduction

Want to follow a ketogenic diet but not sure where to start? Struggling with finding delicious and tummy-filling recipes when going "against the grains"? Do not worry! This book will not only give you 100 amazing keto recipes that will get you started in a jiffy, but it will also teach you the greatest tricks for adopting a keto lifestyle forever.

Mouth-watering delights for any occasion and any eater, you will not believe that these recipes will help you restore your health and slim down your body. Ditching carbs do not mean ditching yummy treats, and with these 100 ingenious recipes, you will see that for yourself.

Successfully practiced for more than nine decades, the ketogenic diet has proven to be the ultimate long-term diet for any person. The restriction list may frighten many, but the truth is, this diet is super adaptable, and the food combinations and tasty meals are pretty endless.

Ketogenic Diet — The New Lifestyle

It is common knowledge that our body is designed to run on carbohydrates. We use them to provide our body with the energy that is required for normal functioning. However, what many people are clueless about, is that carbs are not the only source of fuel that our bodies can use. Just like they can run on carbs, our bodies can also use fats as an energy source. When we ditch the carbs and focus on providing our bodies with more fat, then we are embarking on the ketogenic train.

Despite what many people think, the ketogenic diet is not just another fad diet. It has been around since 1920 and has resulted in outstanding results and amazingly successful stories. If you are new to the keto world, and have no idea what I am talking about, let me simplify this for you.

For you to truly understand what the ketogenic diet is all about and why you should choose to follow it, let me first explain what happens to your body after consuming a carb-loaded meal.

Imagine you have just swallowed a giant bowl of spaghetti. Your tummy is full, your taste buds are satisfied, and your body is provided with much more carbs than necessary. After consumption, your body immediately starts the process of digestion, during which your it will break down the consumed carbs into glucose - the primary source of energy that your body depends on. So one might ask, " What is wrong with carbs?". Well, there are some things. For starters, they raise the blood sugar, they make us fat, and in short, they hurt our overall health. So, how can ketogenic diet help?

A ketogenic diet skips this process by lowering the carbohydrate intake and providing high fat and moderate protein levels. Now, since there is no adequate amount of carbs to use as energy, your liver is forced to find the fuel elsewhere. And since your body is packed with lots of fat, the liver starts using these extra levels of fat as an energy source.

THE KETOSIS

Once your liver begins preparing your body for the fuel change, the fat from the liver will start producing ketones – hence the name ketogenic. What glucose is for the carbs, the ketones are for the fat, meaning that they are the tiny molecules that are created once the fat is broken down to be used as energy.

The switch from glucose to ketones is something that has pushed many people away from this diet. Some people consider this to be a dangerous process, but the truth is, your body will run just as efficiently on ketones, as it does on glucose.

Once your body shifts to using ketones as fuel, you are in the state of *ketosis*. Ketosis is a metabolic process that may be interpreted as a little 'shock' to your body. However, this is far from dangerous. Every change in life requires adaptation, and so does this.

This adaptation process is not set in stone, and every person goes through ketosis differently. However, for most people, it takes around two weeks to adapt to the new lifestyle.

Just remember that this is all biological, and completely normal. You have spent your whole life packing your body with glucose; it is only natural that you also need time to adapt to the new dietary change.

THE BENEFITS

Despite the fact that it is still considered to be 'controversial,' the ketogenic diet is the best dietary choice that one can make. From weight loss to longevity, here are the benefits that following a ketogenic diet can bring to your life:

Loss of Appetite

Cannot tame your cravings? Do not worry. This diet will neither leave you exhausted nor with a rumbling gut. The ketogenic diet will help you say no to that second piece of cake. Once you train your body to run on fat and not on carbs, you will experience a drop in your appetite that will work magic for your figure.

Weight Loss

Since the body is forced to produce only a small amount of glucose, it will also be forced to lower the insulin production. When that happens, your kidneys will start getting rid of the extra sodium, which will lead to weight loss.

HDL Cholesterol Increase

While consuming a diet high in fat and staying clear of the harmful glucose, your body will experience a rise in the good HDL cholesterol levels, which will, in turn, reduce the risk for many cardiovascular problems.

Drop in Blood Pressure

Cutting back on carbs will also bring your blood pressure in check. The drop in the blood pressure can prevent many health problems such as strokes or heart diseases.

Lower Risk of Diabetes

Although this probably goes without saying, it is important to mention this one. When you ditch the carbs, your body is forced to lower the glucose productivity significantly, which naturally leads to a lower risk of diabetes.

Improved Brain Function

Many studies have shown that replacing carbohydrates with fat as an energy source leads to mental clarity and improved brain function. This is yet another reason why you should go keto.

Longevity

I am not saying that this diet will turn you into a 120-hundred-year-old monk; however, it has been scientifically proven that once the oxidative stress levels are lowered, the lifespan gets extended. And since this diet can result in a significant drop in the oxidative stress levels, the corresponding effect it could have on a person's lifespan is evident.

THE KETO PLATE

First, just because it is called a 'diet' doesn't mean that you are about to spend your days in starvation. The ketogenic diet will neither tell you not to eat five times a day if you want to nor will it leave your bellies empty.

The only rule that the keto diet has is to eat fewer carbohydrates, more foods that are high in fat, and consume a moderate protein intake. But how much is too much and what is the right amount? The general rule of a thumb is that your daily nutrition should consist of:

65 - 70 % fat

25 - 30 % protein

3 - 5 % carbohydrates

To be more precise, it is not recommended that you consume more than 20 grams of carbs when on a ketogenic diet.

This macronutrient percentage; however, can be achieved in whichever way you and your belly are comfortable with. For instance, if you crave a carb meal now, and want to eat 16 grams of carbs at once, you can do so, as long as your other meals do not contain more than 4 grams of carbs combined.

Some recipes in this book offer 0 grams of carbs, while others are packed with a few grams. By making a proper meal plan that works for you, you can quickly skip the inconvenience cloaked around this diet, and start receiving the fantastic benefits.

WHAT TO AVOID

For you to stay on track with your Keto diet, there are certain foods that you need to say farewell to. Go to your kitchen and get rid of these tempting but super unhealthy ingredients:

- Sugar

- Diet Soda

- Starchy Vegetables such as potatoes, beans, parsnips, legumes, peas, and corn are usually packed with tons of carbs, so they should be avoided. However, sneaking some starch when your daily carb limit allows, is not exactly a sin.

- Grains — rice, wheat, and everything made from grains such as pasta or bread are not allowed.

- Trans fats

- Refined Oils and Fats (corn oil, canola oil, etc.)

WHAT TO EAT

You can eat anything besides what is mentioned above; however, certain foods will help you up your fat intake and provide you with more longer-lasting energy:

- Meat, Whole Eggs, Fish and Seafood, Bacon, Sausage, Avocados, Leafy Greens

- Non-Starchy Vegetables:

    - Cucumber, Zucchini, Asparagus, Broccoli, Onion, Brussels Sprouts, Cabbage, Tomato, Eggplants, Sea Weed, Peppers, Squash

- Full-Fat Dairy (heavy cream, yogurt, sour cream, cheese, etc.)

- Nuts — nuts are packed with healthy fats, but be careful when consuming pistachios, chestnuts, and cashews, as they contain more carbs than the rest of the nuts. Macadamia nuts, pecans, and almonds are the best for the Keto diet.

- Seeds

KETO SWAPS

Just because you are not allowed to eat rice or pasta, doesn't mean that you have to sacrifice eating risotto or spaghetti. Well, sort of. For every forbidden item on the keto diet, there is a healthier replacement that will not contradict your dietary goal and will still taste amazing.

Here are the ultimate keto swaps that you need to know of to overcome the cravings quicker, and become a Keto chef:

Bread and Buns → Bread made from nut flour, mushroom caps, cucumber slices

Wraps and tortillas → Wraps and tortillas made from nut flour, lettuce leaves, kale leaves

Pasta and spaghetti → Spiralized veggies such as zoodles, spaghetti squash, etc.

Lasagna Noodles → Zucchini or eggplant slices

Rice → Cauliflower rice (ground in a food processor)

Mashed potatoes → Mashed cauliflower or other veggies

Hash browns → Cauliflower or spaghetti squash

Flour → Coconut flour, nut flour

Breadcrumbs → Almond Flour

Pizza crust → Crust made with allowed flour, cauliflower crust

French fries → Carrot sticks, turnip fries, zucchini fries

Potato Chips → Zucchini chips, kale chips

Croutons → Bacon bits, nuts, sunflower seeds, flax crackers

Squash and Sausage Omelet with Kale

Serves: 1 / Preparation + Cook Time: 10 minutes

Nutritional Info:

Calories 258, Net Carbs 3.55 g, Fat 21.7 g, Protein 12.3 g

Ingredients:

2 Eggs

1 cup of Kale, chopped

4 oz. Sausage, chopped

2 tbsp. Ricotta Cheese

4 ounces Roasted Squash

1 tbsp. Olive Oil

Fresh parsley to garnish

Preparation:

1. Beat the eggs in a bowl and stir in the kale and the ricotta.
2. In another bowl, mash the squash.
3. Add the squash to the egg mixture.
4. Heat ¼ tbsp. of olive oil in a pan over medium heat.
5. Add sausage and cook until browned on all sides.
6. Drizzle the remaining olive oil. Pour the egg mixture over.
7. Cook for about 2 minutes per side.
8. Serve sprinkled with fresh parsley.

Sausage Quiche with Tomatoes

Serves: 6 / Preparation + Cook Time: 55 minutes

Nutritional Info:

Calories 340, Net Carbs 3 g, Fat 28 g, Protein 1.7 g

Ingredients:

6 Eggs

12 ounces Raw Sausage Roll

10 Cherry Tomatoes, halved

2 tbsp. Heavy Cream

2 tbsp. Parmesan Cheese

¼ tsp Salt

Pinch of Black Pepper

2 tbsp. chopped Parsley

5 Eggplant Slices

Preparation:

1. Preheat your oven to 375 degrees F.
2. Press the sausage roll at the bottom of a pie dish (preferably an 8-inch one).
3. Arrange the eggplant slices on top of the sausage.
4. Top with cherry tomatoes.
5. Whisk together the eggs along with the heavy cream, salt, parmesan, and pepper. Pour the egg mixture over the sausage.
6. Bake for about 40 minutes.
7. Serve warm and scatter with chopped parsley.

Italian Omelet

Serves: 1 / Preparation + Cook Time: 15 minutes

Nutritional Info:

Calories 451, Net Carbs 3 g, Fat 36.5 g, Protein 30 g

Ingredients:

2 Eggs

6 basil Leaves

2 ounces Mozzarella

1 tbsp. Butter

1 tbsp. Water

5-8 thin slices Chorizo

5 thin slices Tomato (1 tomato)

Salt and Pepper, to taste

Preparation:

1. Whisk the eggs along with the water and some salt and pepper.
2. Melt the butter in a skillet and cook the eggs for 30 seconds.
3. Spread the meat slices over.
4. Arrange the sliced tomato and mozzarella around the chorizo and pour the egg mixture.
5. Cook for about 2 minutes per side.
6. Cover the skillet and cook for 1 more minute.
7. Serve garnished with basil leaves.

Ham and Egg Cups

Serves: 9 / Preparation + Cook Time: 40 minutes

Nutritional Info:

Calories 267, Net Carbs 1 g, Fat 18 g, Protein 13.5 g

Ingredients:

2 cups chopped Ham

⅓ cup grated Parmesan Cheese

1 tbsp. chopped Parsley

¼ cup Almond Flour

9 Eggs

⅓ cup Mayonnaise, sugar-free

¼ tsp Garlic Powder

¼ cup chopped Onion

Sea salt to taste

Preparation:

1. Preheat your oven to 375 degrees F.
2. Place the onion, ham, garlic powder, and salt, in a food processor, and pulse until ground.
3. Stir in the mayonnaise, almond flour, and Parmesan cheese.
4. Press this mixture into nine muffin cups. Make sure it goes all the way up the muffin sides, so that there will be room for the egg.
5. Bake for 5 minutes.
6. Crack an egg into each muffin cup.
7. Return to the oven and bake for 20 more minutes.

Breakfast Hash with Bacon and Zucchini

Serves: 1 / Preparation + Cook Time: 25 minutes

Nutritional Info:

Calories 423, Net Carbs 6.6 g, Fat 35.5 g, Protein 17.4 g

Ingredients:

1 Medium Zucchini, chopped

2 Bacon Slices

1 Egg

1 tbsp. Coconut Oil

½ small Onion, chopped

1 tbsp. chopped Parsley

¼ tsp Salt

Preparation:

1. Place the bacon and onion in a skillet and cook over medium heat for a few minutes, until the onion becomes soft and the bacon is crispy.
2. Add the zucchini in the skillet and cook for 10 more minutes.
3. Transfer to a bowl. Season with salt.
4. Crack the egg into the same skillet and fry it over medium heat.
5. Top the zucchini mixture with the fried egg. Serve sprinkled with parsley.

Quick Breakfast Porridge

Serves: 1 / Preparation + Cook Time: 10 minutes

Nutritional Info:

Calories 334, Net Carbs 1.5 g, Fat 29 g, Protein 15 g

Ingredients:

½ tsp Vanilla Extract

½ cup Water

1 tbsp. Chia Seeds

2 tbsp. Hemp Seeds

1 tbsp. Flaxseed Meal	2 tbsp. Shredded Coconut
2 tbsp. Almond Meal	¼ tsp Granulated Stevia

Preparation:

1. Combine all ingredients (except the vanilla extract) in a saucepan, and place over medium heat.
2. Simmer for about 3-4 minutes or until thickened. Stir in vanilla.

Almond Butter Shake

Serves: 1 / Preparation + Cook Time: 2 minutes

Nutritional Info:

Calories 326, Net Carbs 6 g, Fat 27 g, Protein 19 g

Ingredients:

1 ½ cup Almond Milk
2 tbsp. Almond Butter
⅛ tsp Almond Extract
½ tsp Cinnamon
2 tbsp. Flax Meal
1 scoop Collagen Peptides
Pinch of Salt
15 drops of Stevia
A handful of Ice Cubes

Preparation:

1. Place all of the ingredients in the bowl of your blender.
2. Blend until smooth, for about 30 seconds.
3. Drink immediately.

Pesto Mug Muffin Sandwich with Bacon and Cream Cheese

Serves: 2 / Preparation + Cook Time: 5 minutes

Nutritional Info:

Calories 511, Net Carbs 4.5 g, Fat 38.2 g, Protein 16.4 g

Ingredients:

¼ cup Flax Meal

1 Egg

2 tbsp. Heavy Cream

2 tbsp. Pesto

¼ cup Almond Flour

¼ tsp Baking Soda

Salt and ground black pepper, to taste

Filling:

2 tbsp. Cream Cheese

4 sliced of Bacon

½ medium Avocado, sliced

Preparation:

1. Mix together the muffin ingredients in a bowl. Season with salt and pepper. Divide the mixture between two ramekins.
2. Place in the microwave and cook for 60-90 seconds.
3. Invert the muffins onto a plate and cut in crosswise.
4. Assemble the sandwiches by spreading cream cheese and topping with bacon and avocado slices.

Herbed Buttered Eggs

Serves: 2 / Preparation + Cook Time: 15 minutes

Nutritional Info:

Calories 321, Net Carbs 2.5 g, Fat 21.5 g, Protein 12.8 g

Ingredients:

1 tbsp. Coconut Oil

2 tbsp. Butter

1 tsp fresh Thyme

4 Eggs

2 Garlic Cloves, minced

½ cup chopped Parsley

½ cup chopped Cilantro

¼ tsp Cumin

¼ tsp Cayenne Pepper

Salt and ground black pepper, to taste

Preparation:

1. Melt the butter and coconut oil together in a skillet over medium heat.
2. Add garlic and cook for 30 seconds.
3. Add thyme and bake for 30 more seconds.
4. Sprinkle with parsley and cilantro, and cook for another 2-3 minutes, until crisp.
5. Crack the eggs into the skillet.
6. Lower the heat and cook for 4-6 minutes.
7. Adjust the seasoning and serve warm.

Feta and Spinach Frittata with Cherry Tomatoes

Serves: 4 / Preparation + Cook Time: 40 minutes

Nutritional Info:

Calories 461, Net Carbs 6 g, Fat 35 g, Protein 26 g

Ingredients:

5 ounces Spinach

8 ounces crumbled Feta Cheese

1 pint halved Cherry Tomatoes

10 Eggs

3 tbsp. Olive Oil

4 Scallions, diced

Salt and pepper, to taste

Fresh Parsley, to garnish

Preparation:

1. Preheat your oven to 350 degrees F.
2. Drizzle the oil in a 2-quart casserole and place in the oven until heated.
3. In a bowl, whisk the eggs along with the pepper and salt.
4. Stir in the rest of the ingredients.
5. Pour the mixture in the casserole and place back in the oven.
6. Bake for 25 minutes.
7. Let cool the frittata in the casserole for 5-6 minutes, then sprinkle with parsley.
8. Serve sliced into wedges.

Omelet Wrap with Avocado and Salmon

Serves: 1 / Preparation + Cook Time: 15 minutes

Nutritional Info:

Calories 514, Net Carbs 5.8 g, Fat 47.9 g, Protein 36.9 g

Ingredients:

½ Avocado, sliced

2 tbsp. chopped Chives

½ package smoked Salmon (about 1.8 ounces), cut into strips

1 Spring Onion, sliced

3 Eggs

2 tbsp. Cream Cheese

1 tbsp. Butter

Salt and pepper, to taste

Preparation:

1. In a small bowl, combine the chives and cream cheese. Set aside.

2. Melt the butter in a pan over medium heat.

3. Add the eggs and cook for about 2 minutes per side.

4. Place the omelet in a plate and spread the chive mixture over. Season with salt and pepper to taste.

5. Arrange the salmon, avocado, and onion slices. Wrap the omelet.

Cheddar and Broccoli Soup

Serves: 4 / Preparation + Cook Time: 20 minutes

Nutritional Info:

Calories 561, Net Carbs 7 g, Fat 52.3 g, Protein 23.8 g

Ingredients:

¾ cup Heavy Cream

1 Onion, diced

1 tsp minced Garlic

4 cups chopped Broccoli

4 cups Veggie Broth

2 ¾ cups grated Cheddar Cheese + ¼ cup to garnish

Salt and Pepper, to taste

½ bunch Fresh Mint, chopped

Preparation:

1. Combine the broth, broccoli, onion, and garlic, in a large pot.

2. Place over medium heat and bring to a boil.

3. Reduce the heat and simmer for 10 minutes.

4. Blend the soup with a hand blender until smooth.

5. Stir in the heavy cream and cook for another 2 minutes.

6. Add in the cheese and cook until smooth, about 1 minute.

7. Taste, season with salt and pepper and serve in bowls with the reserved grated Cheddar cheese over and sprinkled with the fresh mint. Yummy!

Chicken Enchilada Soup

Serves: 4 / Preparation + Cook Time: 15 minutes

Nutritional Info:

Calories 346, Net Carbs 3 g, Fat 23 g, Protein 25 g

Ingredients:

½ cup Salsa Enchilada Verde

2 cups cooked and shredded Chicken

2 cups Chicken or Bone Broth

1 cup shredded Cheddar Cheese

4 ounces Cream Cheese

½ tsp chili powder

½ tsp ground cumin

½ tsp fresh cilantro, chopped

Salt and ground black pepper, to taste

Preparation:

1. Combine the cream cheese, salsa verde, and broth, in a food processor.

2. Pulse until smooth. Transfer the mixture to a pot and place over medium heat. Cook until hot, but do not bring to a boil.

3. Add chicken, chili powder, and cumin and cook for about 3-5 minutes, or until it is heated through. Stir in Cheddar cheese. Season with salt and pepper to taste.

Tip: If it is very thick, add a few tablespoons of water and boil for 1-3 more minutes.

4. Serve hot in individual bowls sprinkled with fresh cilantro.

Slow Cooked Sausage Soup with Beer and Cheddar

Serves: 8 / Preparation + Cook Time: 8 hours

Nutritional Info:

Calories 244, Net Carbs 4 g, Fat 17 g, Protein 5 g

Ingredients:

1 cup Heavy Cream

10 ounces Beef Sausages, sliced

1 cup chopped Celery

1 cup chopped Carrots

4 Garlic Cloves, minced

8 ounces Cream Cheese

1 tsp Red Pepper Flakes

6 ounces Beer

16 ounces Beef Stock

1 Onion, diced

1 cups Cheddar Cheese

Salt and ground black pepper, to taste

Fresh cilantro, chopped, to garnish

Preparation:

1. Heat the slow cooker on Low. Add broth, beer, sausage, carrots, onion, celery, salt, red pepper flakes, salt, and pepper, and stir to combine.
2. Add enough water to cover all the ingredients by roughly 2 inches. Close the lid and cook for 6 hours.
3. Open the lid and stir in the heavy cream, cheddar, and cream cheese, and cook for 2 more hours.
4. Ladle the soup into bowls and garnish with cilantro before serving.

Shrimp Stew

Serves: 6 / Preparation + Cook Time: 25 minutes

Nutritional Info:

Calories 324, Net Carbs 5 g, Fat 21 g, Protein 23.1 g

Ingredients:

1 cup Milk

2 tbsp. Lime Juice

¼ cup diced Roasted Peppers

1 ½ pounds Shrimp, peeled and deveined

¼ cup Olive Oil

1 Garlic Clove, minced

14 ounces diced Tomatoes

2 tbsp. Sriracha Sauce

¼ cup chopped Onions

¼ cup chopped Cilantro

Fresh dill, chopped to garnish

Salt and ground black pepper, to taste

Preparation:

1. Heat the olive oil in a pot over medium heat.

2. Add onions and cook for 3 minutes.

3. Add the garlic and cook for another minute, until tender. Add tomatoes, shrimp, and cilantro.

4. Cook until the shrimp becomes opaque, about 3-4 minutes.

5. Stir in sriracha and milk, and cook for 2 more minutes. Do NOT bring to a boil. Stir in the lime juice and season with salt and pepper to taste.

6. Spoon the stew in bowls, garnish with fresh dill and serve warm.

Chorizo and Cauliflower Soup

Serves: 4 / Preparation + Cook Time: 30 minutes

Nutritional Info:

Calories 251, Net Carbs 5.7 g, Fat 19.1 g, Protein 10 g

Ingredients:

1 Cauliflower Head, chopped

1 Turnip, chopped

3 tbsp. Butter

1 Chorizo Sausage, sliced

2 cups Chicken Broth

1 small Onion, chopped

2 cups water

Salt and ground black pepper, to taste

Preparation:

1. Melt 2 tbsp. of the butter in a large pot over medium heat.

2. Stir in onions and cook until soft, about 3 minutes.

3. Add cauliflower and turnip, and cook for another 5 minutes.

4. Pour the broth and water over. Bring to a boil, and simmer covered, and cook for about 10 minutes.

5. Remove from heat. Melt the remaining butter in a skillet.

6. Add the chorizo and cook for 5 minutes.

7. Stir of the chorizo into the soup, and blend with a hand blender until smooth. Taste and adjust the seasonings.

8. Serve the soup topped with the remaining chorizo.

Wild Mushroom Soup

Serves: 4 / Preparation + Cook Time: 25 minutes

Nutritional Info:

Calories 281, Net Carbs 5.8 g, Fat 25 g, Protein 6.1 g

Ingredients:

¼ cup Butter

5 ounces Crème Fraiche

12 ounces Wild Mushrooms, chopped

2 tsp Thyme Leaves, to serve

2 Garlic Cloves, minced

4 cups Chicken Broth

Salt and ground black pepper, to taste

Preparation:

1. Melt the butter in a large pot over medium heat.

2. Add garlic and cook for one minute until tender.

3. Add mushrooms, season with salt and pepper, and cook for 5-10 minutes.

4. Pour the broth over and bring to a boil.

5. Reduce the heat and simmer for 10 minutes.

6. Blend the mixture with a hand blender until smooth.

7. Stir in crème Fraiche.

8. Garnish with thyme leaves when serving.

Pork and Pumpkin Stew with Peanuts

Serves: 6 / Preparation + Cook Time: 45 minutes

Nutritional Info:

Calories 451, Net Carbs 4 g, Fat 33 g, Protein 27.5 g

Ingredients:

1 cup Pumpkin Puree

2 pounds chopped Pork

1 tbsp. Peanut Butter

4 tbsp. chopped Peanuts

1 Garlic Clove, minced

½ cup chopped Onion

½ cup White Wine

1 tbsp. Olive Oil

1 tsp Lemon Juice

¼ cup Granulated Sweetener

¼ tsp Cardamom

¼ tsp All Spice

2 cups water

2 cups chicken stock

Preparation:

1. Heat the olive oil in a large pot. Add onions and cook for 3 minutes until translucent. Add garlic and cook for 30 more seconds.
2. Add the pork and cook until browned, about 3 minutes per side. Pour in the wine and cook for one minute.
3. Stir in the remaining ingredients, except lemon juice and peanuts.
4. Bring the mixture to a boil, and cook for 5 minutes.

5. Reduce the heat to low, cover the pot, and let cook for about 30 minutes.

6. Stir in the lemon juice before serving.

7. Serve topped with peanuts and enjoy.

Creamy Chicken Soup

Serves: 4 / Preparation + Cook Time: 15 minutes

Nutritional Info:

Calories 406, Net Carbs 5 g, Fat 29.5 g, Protein 26.5 g

Ingredients:

2 cups cooked and shredded Chicken

3 tbsp. Butter, melted

½ cup and

4 cups Chicken Broth

4 tbsp. chopped Cilantro, to garnish

⅓ cup Buffalo Sauce

4 ounces Cream Cheese

Salt and pepper, to taste

Preparation:

1. Blend the butter, buffalo sauce, and cream cheese, in a food processor until uniform and smooth.

2. Transfer to a pot, add the chicken broth and heat until hot but do not bring to a boil.

3. Stir in chicken and cook until heated through.

4. Taste, adjust the seasoning and serve warm garnished with cilantro.

Red Gazpacho

Serves: 6 / Preparation + Cook Time: 15 minutes

Nutritional Info:

Calories 528, Net Carbs 8.5 g, Fat 45.8 g, Protein 7.5 g

Ingredients:

2 small Green Peppers, roasted

2 large Red Peppers, roasted

2 Medium Avocados, flesh scoped out

2 Garlic Cloves

2 Spring Onions, chopped

1 Cucumber, chopped

1 cup Olive Oil

2 tbsp. Lemon Juice

4 Tomatoes, chopped

7 ounces Goat Cheese

1 small Red Onion, coarsely chopped

2 tbsp. Apple Cider Vinegar

Salt to taste

Preparation:

1. Chop all of the veggies, and scoop out the avocado flesh.
2. Place the peppers, tomatoes, avocado, onion, garlic, lemon juice, olive oil, vinegar, and salt, in a food processor or a blender. Pulse until your desired consistency is reached. Taste and adjust the seasoning as necessary.
3. Transfer the mixture to a pot. Stir in cucumbers and green onions. Cover and chill in the fridge at least 2 hours.
4. Divide the soup between 6 bowls. Serve very cold, generously topped with goat cheese and an extra drizzle of olive oil.

Keto Reuben Soup

Serves: 7 / Preparation + Cook Time: 20 minutes

Nutritional Info:

Calories 450, Net Carbs 8 g, Fat 37 g, Protein 23 g

Ingredients:

1 Onion, diced

4 cups Beef Stock

1 tsp Caraway Seeds

2 Celery Stalks, diced

2 Garlic Cloves, minced

¾ tsp Black Pepper

2 cups Heavy Cream

1 cup Sauerkraut

1 pound Corned Beef, chopped

3 tbsp. Butter

1 ½ cup Swiss Cheese

Salt and pepper, to taste

Preparation:

1. Melt the butter in a large pot. Add onions and celery, and cook for 3 minutes. Add garlic and cook for another minute.

2. Pour the broth over and stir in sauerkraut, salt, caraway seeds, and pepper. Bring to a boil. Reduce the heat to low, and add the corned beef.

3. Cook for about 15 minutes. Season with salt and pepper.

4. Stir in heavy cream and cheese and cook for 1 minute.

Tip: For more protein add some cooked and chopped shrimp to this refreshing delight.

Superfood and Low-Protein Soup

Serves: 6 / Preparation + Cook Time: 30 minutes

Nutritional Info:

Calories 392, Net Carbs 5.8 g, Fat 37.6 g, Protein 4.9 g

Ingredients:

1 Broccoli head, chopped

7 ounces Spinach

1 Onion, chopped

2 Garlic Cloves, minced

5 ounces Watercress

4 cups Veggie Stock

1 cup Coconut Milk

1 tsp Salt

1 tbsp. Ghee

1 Bay Leaf

Salt and ground black pepper, to taste

Preparation:

1. Melt the ghee in a large pot over medium heat.
2. Add onion and cook for 3 minutes. Add garlic and cook for another minute.
3. Add broccoli and cook for additional 5 minutes.
4. Pour the stock over and add the bay leaf.
5. Close the lid, bring to a boil, and reduce the heat.
6. Simmer for about 3 minutes.
7. In the end, add spinach and watercress, and cook for 3 more minutes.
8. Stir in the coconut cream and salt and pepper.
9. Discard the bay leaf, and blend the soup with a hand blender.

Salads

Goat Cheese Salad Bowl with Spinach and Strawberries

Serves: 2 / Preparation + Cook Time: 20 minutes

Nutritional Info:

Calories 645, Net Carbs 5.8 g, Fat 54.2 g, Protein 33 g

Ingredients:

4 cups Spinach

4 Strawberries, sliced

½ cup flaked Almonds

1 ½ cup grated hard Goat Cheese

4 tbsp. Raspberry Vinaigrette

Salt and pepper, to taste

Preparation:

1. Preheat your oven to 400 degrees F.
2. Arrange the grated goat cheese in two circles on two pieces of parchment paper. Place in the oven and bake for 10 minutes.
3. Find two same bowls, place them upside down, and carefully put the parchment paper on top of them, to give the cheese a bowl-like shape.
4. Let cool that way for 15 minutes.
5. Divide the spinach between two bowls.
6. Drizzle the vinaigrette over.
7. Top with almond and strawberries.

Mackerel and Green Beans Salad

Serves: 2 / Preparation + Cook Time: 25 minutes

Nutritional Info:

Calories 525, Net Carbs 7.6 g, Fat 41.9 g, Protein 27.3 g

Ingredients:

2 Mackerel Fillets

2 Hardboiled Eggs, sliced

1 tbsp. Coconut Oil

2 cups Green Beans

1 Avocado, sliced

4 cups mixed Salad Greens

2 tbsp. Olive Oil

2 tbsp. Lemon Juice

1 tsp Dijon Mustard

Salt and pepper, to taste

Preparation:

1. Fill a saucepan with water and add the beans and some salt.
2. Cook over medium heat for about 3 minutes. Drain and set aside.
3. Melt the coconut oil in a pan over medium heat.
4. Add the mackerel fillets and cook for about 4 minutes per side, or until opaque and crispy.
5. Divide the greens between two serving bowls. Top with mackerel, egg, and avocado sliced.
6. In a separate bowl, whisk together the lemon juice, olive oil, mustard, salt, and pepper, and drizzle over the salad.

Low-Protein Artichoke Salad

Serves: 4 / Preparation + Cook Time: 35 minutes

Nutritional Info:

Calories 170, Net Carbs 5 g, Fat 13 g, Protein 1 g

Ingredients:

6 Baby Artichokes

6 cups Water

1 tbsp. Lemon Juice

¼ cup Cherry Peppers, halved

¼ cup pitted Olives, sliced

¼ cup Olive Oil

¼ tsp Lemon Zest

2 tsp Balsamic Vinegar, sugar-free

1 tbsp. chopped Dill

½ tsp Salt

¼ tsp Black Pepper

1 tbsp. Capers

¼ tsp Caper Brine

Preparation:

1. Combine the water and salt in a pot over medium heat. Trim and halve the artichokes and add to the pot. Bring to a boil, lower the heat, and let simmer for 20 minutes until tender.

2. Meanwhile, combine the rest of the ingredients, except the olives in a bowl.

3. Drain and place the artichokes in a serving plate.

4. Pour the prepared mixture over. Toss to combine well.

5. Serve topped with the olives.

Chicken Caesar Salad with Bok Choy

Serves: 4 / Preparation + Cook Time: 1 hour and 30 minutes

Nutritional Info:

Calories 529, Net Carbs 5 g, Fat 39 g, Protein 33 g

Ingredients:

Chicken:

4 Boneless and Skinless Chicken Thighs

¼ cup Lemon Juice

2 Garlic Cloves, minced

2 tbsp. Olive Oil

Salt and pepper, to taste

Salad:

½ cup Caesar Salad Dressing, sugar-free

2 tbsp. Olive Oil

12 Bok Choy Leaves

3 Parmesan Crisps

Grated Parmesan Cheese, for garnishing

Preparation:

1. Combine the chicken ingredients in a Ziploc bag,
2. Seal the bag, shake to combine, and refrigerate for 1 hour.
3. Preheat the grill to medium heat and grill the chicken about 4 minutes per side.
4. Cut the bok choy leaves lengthwise, and brush it with olive oil.
5. Grill the bok choy for about 3 minutes. Place on a serving platter.
6. Top with the chicken and drizzle the dressing over.
7. Scatter grated parmesan cheese over and serve.

Lobster Roll Salad

Serves: 4 / Preparation + Cook Time: 1 hour 10 minutes

Nutritional Info:

Calories 182, Net Carbs 2 g, Fat 15 g, Protein 12 g

Ingredients:

5 cups Cauliflower Florets

⅓ cup diced Celery

½ cup sliced Black Olives

2 cups cooked large Shrimp

1 tbsp. Dill, chopped

Dressing:

½ cup Mayonnaise

1 tsp Apple Cider Vinegar

¼ tsp Celery Seed

A pinch of Black Pepper

2 tbsp. Lemon Juice

2 tsp Swerve sweetener

Preparation:

1. Combine all of the salad ingredients in a large bowl.

2. Whisk together the dressing ingredients in another bowl.

3. Pour the dressing over the salad. Mix to combine well.

4. Refrigerate for one hour. Serve cold and enjoy!

Bacon and Avocado Salad

Serves: 4 / Preparation + Cook Time: 20 minutes

Nutritional Info:

Calories 350, Net Carbs 3.4 g, Fat 33 g, Protein 7 g

Ingredients:

2 Large Avocados, 1 chopped and 1 sliced

1 Spring Onion, sliced

4 Bacon Slices, crumbled

2 cups Spinach

2 small Lettuce Heads, chopped

2 Hardboiled Eggs, chopped

Vinaigrette:

3 tbsp. Olive Oil

1 tsp Dijon Mustard

1 tbsp. Apple Cider Vinegar

Preparation:

1. Heat a nonstick skillet over medium heat and cook the bacon until crispy. Drain on a paper towel; set aside.
2. Combine the spinach, lettuce, eggs, chopped avocados, and spring onion, in a large bowl.
3. Whisk together the vinaigrette ingredients in another bowl.
4. Pour the dressing over. Toss to combine.
5. Top with the sliced avocado and bacon.

Shrimp Salad with Cauliflower and Cucumber

Serves: 6 / Preparation + Cook Time: 30 minutes

Nutritional Info:

Calories 214, Net Carbs 5 g, Fat 17 g, Protein 15 g

Ingredients:

1 Cauliflower Head, florets only

1 pound Medium Shrimp

¼ cup plus 1 tbsp. Olive Oil

2 Cucumber, peeled and chopped

3 tbsp. chopped Dill

¼ cup Lemon Juice

2 tbsp. Lemon Zest

Salt and pepper, to taste

Fresh dill, to serve

Preparation:

1. Heat 1 tbsp. olive oil in a skillet and cook the shrimp until opaque, about 8-10 minutes.

2. Place the cauliflower florets in a microwave-safe bowl, and microwave for 5 minutes until tender.

3. Place the shrimp, cauliflower, and cucumber in a large bowl.

4. Whisk together the remaining olive oil, lemon zest, juice, dill, and some salt and pepper, in another bowl.

5. Pour the dressing over. Toss to combine.

6. Serve sprinkled with fresh dill.

Caprese Salad with Bacon

Serves: 2 / Preparation + Cook Time: 10 minutes

Nutritional Info:

Calories 279, Net Carbs 1.5 g, Fat 26 g, Protein 21 g

Ingredients:

1 Large Tomato, sliced

4 Basil Leaves

8 Mozzarella Cheese Slices

2 tsp Olive Oil

3 ounces Bacon, chopped

1 tsp Balsamic Vinegar

Preparation:

1. Place the bacon in a skillet over medium heat and cook until crispy.

2. Divide the tomato slices between two serving platters.

3. Arrange the mozzarella slices over. Top with the basil leaves.

4. Add the crispy bacon on top.

5. Drizzle with olive oil and vinegar.

Quick and Easy Tuna Salad

Serves: 2 / Preparation + Cook Time: 5 minutes

Nutritional Info:

Calories 248, Net Carbs 2 g, Fat 20 g, Protein 18.5 g

Ingredients:

1 cup Canned Tuna, drained

1 tsp Onion Flakes

3 tbsp. Mayonnaise

1 cup shredded Romaine Lettuce

Preparation:

1. Place the tuna, onion, mayonnaise, and salt to taste in a large bowl.

2. Mix to combine well.

3. Serve on lettuce bed.

Classic Greek Salad

Serves: 4 / Preparation + Cook Time: 10 minutes

Nutritional Info:

Calories 323, Net Carbs 8 g, Fat 28 g, Protein 9.3 g

Ingredients:

5 Tomatoes, chopped
1 Large Cucumber, chopped
1 Green Bell Pepper, chopped
1 small Red Onion, chopped
16 Kalamata Olives, chopped
4 tbsp. Capers
7 ounces Feta Cheese, chopped
1 tsp Oregano, dried
4 tbsp. Olive Oil
Salt to taste

Preparation:

1. Place tomatoes, pepper, cucumber, onion, feta and olives in a bowl.

2. Mix to combine well. Season with salt.

3. Combine the capers, olive oil, and oregano, in a small bowl.

4. Drizzle the dressing over the salad.

Mayo and Broccoli Slaw

Serves: 6 / Preparation + Cook Time: 10 minutes

Nutritional Info:

Calories 110, Net Carbs 2 g, Fat 10 g, Protein 3 g

Ingredients:

2 tbsp. powdered granular sweetener

1 tbsp. Dijon Mustard

1 tbsp. Olive Oil

4 cups Broccoli Slaw

⅓ cup Mayonnaise, sugar-free

1 tsp Celery Seeds

1 ½ tbsp. Apple Cider Vinegar

Salt and pepper, to taste

Preparation:

1. Whisk together the mayonnaise, mustard, sweetener, olive oil, celery seeds, vinegar until everything is well combined.
2. Season to taste with salt and pepper.
3. Place broccoli in a large salad bowl.
4. Pour the dressing over.
5. Mix with your hands to combine well.
6. Serve immediately

Simple Italian Tricolore Salad

Serves: 4 / Preparation + Cook Time: 10 minutes

Nutritional Info:

Calories 290, Net Carbs 4.3 g, Fat 25 g, Protein 9 g

Ingredients:

3 Tomatoes, sliced

1 Large Avocado, sliced

8 Kalamata Olives

¼ pound Buffalo Mozzarella Cheese, sliced

2 tbsp. Pesto Sauce

2 tbsp. Olive Oil

Preparation:

1. Arrange the tomato slices on a serving platter.
2. Place the avocado slices in the middle.
3. Arrange the olives around the avocado slices.
4. Drop pieces of mozzarella on the platter.
5. Top with the pesto sauce.
6. Drizzle with the olive oiland serve.

Spinach Cheesy Puff Balls

Serves: 8 / Preparation + Cook Time: 30 minutes

Nutritional Info:

Calories 60, Net Carbs 0.8 g, Fat 5 g, Protein 2 g

Ingredients:

⅓ cup crumbled Ricotta Cheese

¼ tsp Nutmeg

¼ tsp Pepper

3 tbsp. Heavy Cream

1 tsp Garlic Powder

1 tbsp. Onion Powder

2 tbsp. Butter, melted

⅓ cup Parmesan Cheese

2 Eggs

8 ounces Spinach

1 cup Almond Flour

Preparation:

1. Place all of the ingredients in a food processor. Process until smooth.
2. Place in the freezer for about 10 minutes.
3. Make balls out of the mixture and arrange them on a lined baking sheet.
4. Bake at 350 degrees F for about 10-12 minutes.

Goat Cheese Stuffed Peppers

Serves: 8 / Preparation + Cook Time: 20 minutes

Nutritional Info:

Calories 110, Net Carbs 2.5 g, Fat 9 g, Protein 6 g

Ingredients:

8 canned Roasted Piquillo Peppers

1 tbsp. Olive Oil

3 slices Prosciutto, cut into thin slices

1 tbsp. Balsamic Vinegar

Filling:

8 ounces Goat Cheese

3 tbsp. Heavy Cream

3 tbsp. chopped Parsley

½ tsp minced Garlic

1 tbsp. Olive Oil

1 tbsp. chopped Mint

Preparation:

1. Combine all of the filling ingredients in a bowl.
2. Place the mixture in a freezer bag, press down and squeeze, and cut off the bottom. Drain and deseed the peppers.
3. Squeeze about 2 tbsp. of the filling into each pepper.
4. Wrap a prosciutto slice onto each pepper. Secure with toothpicks.
5. Arrange them on a serving platter. Sprinkle the olive oil and vinegar over.

Crispy and Cheesy Salami

Serves: 6 / Preparation + Cook Time: 30 minutes

Nutritional Info:

Calories 27, Net Carbs 0 g, Fat 3 g, Protein 2 g

Ingredients:

7 ounces dried Salami

4 ounces Cream Cheese

¼ cup chopped Parsley

Preparation:

1. Preheat your oven to 325 degrees F. Slice the Salami into 30 slices
2. Line a baking dish with waxed paper. Bake the salami for 15 minutes until crispy.
3. Remove from the oven and let cool.
4. Arrange on a serving platter. Top each slice with some cream cheese.
5. Serve with sprinkled with chopped parsley.

Butter-Drowned Broccoli

Serves: 6 / Preparation + Cook Time: 10 minutes

Nutritional Info:

Calories 114, Net Carbs 5.5 g, Fat 7.8 g, Protein 3.9 g

Ingredients:

1 Broccoli Head, florets only

¼ cup Butter

Salt

Preparation:

1. Place the broccoli in a pot filled with salted water and bring to a boil.
2. Cook for about 3 minutes, or until tender.
3. Meanwhile, melt the butter in a microwave. Drain the broccoli and transfer to a plate.
4. Drizzle the butter over and season with some salt and pepper.

Fried Artichoke Hearts

Serves: 4 / Preparation + Cook Time: 20 minutes

Nutritional Info:

Calories 35, Net Carbs 2.9 g, Fat 2.4 g, Protein 2 g

Ingredients:

12 Fresh Baby Artichokes
2 tbsp. Lemon Juice
Olive Oil
Salt

Preparation:

1. Slice the artichokes vertically into narrow wedges. Drain them on paper towels before frying.
2. Heat olive oil in a cast-iron skillet over high heat.
3. Fry the artichokes until browned and crispy. Place on paper towels to soak up excess oil.
4. Sprinkle with salt and lemon juice.

Basic Cauliflower Fritters

Serves: 4 / Preparation + Cook Time: 35 minutes

Nutritional Info:

Calories 69, Net Carbs 3 g, Fat 4.5 g, Protein 4.5 g

Ingredients:

1 pound grated Cauliflower

½ cup Parmesan Cheese

3 ounces finely chopped Onion

½ tsp Baking Powder

½ cup Almond Flour

3 Eggs

1 ½ tsp Lemon Pepper

Olive Oil, for frying

Preparation:

1. Sprinkle the salt over the cauliflower in a bowl, and let it stand for 10 minutes. Place the other ingredients in the bowl. Mix with your hands to combine. Place a skillet over medium heat, and heat some olive oil in it.

2. Meanwhile, shape fritters out of the cauliflower mixture.

3. Fry in batches, for about 3 minutes per side.

Keto Deviled Eggs

Serves: 6 / Preparation + Cook Time: 30 minutes

Nutritional Info:

Calories 178, Net Carbs 5 g, Fat 17 g, Protein 6 g

Ingredients:

6 Eggs

1 tbsp. Green Tabasco

⅓ cup Sugar-Free Mayonnaise

Preparation:

1. Place the eggs in a saucepan and cover with salted water. Bring to a boil over medium heat. Boil for 8 minutes. Place the eggs in an ice bath and let cool for 10 minutes. Peel and slice them in .
2. Whisk together the tabasco, mayonnaise, and salt, in a small bowl.
3. Spoon this mixture on top of every egg .

Provolone and Prosciutto Chicken Wraps

Serves: 8 / Preparation + Cook Time: 20 minutes

Nutritional Info:

Calories 174, Net Carbs 0.75 g, Fat 10 g, Protein 17 g

Ingredients:

¼ tsp Garlic Powder

8 ounces Provolone Cheese

8 Raw Chicken Tenders

⅛ tsp Black Pepper

8 Prosciutto Slices

Preparation:

1. Pound the chicken until an inch thick. Season with salt, pepper, and garlic powder. Cut the provolone cheese into 8 strips.
2. Place a slice of prosciutto on a flat surface. Place one chicken tender on top. Top with a provolone strip.
3. Roll the chicken and secure with previously soaked skewers.
4. Grill the wraps for about 3 minutes per side.

Tuna Topped Pickles

Serves: 12 / Preparation + Cook Time: 40 minutes

Nutritional Info:

Calories 118, Net Carbs 1.5 g, Fat 10 g, Protein 11 g

Ingredients:

12 ounces canned and drained Tuna

6 large Dill Pickles

6 ounces canned smoky Tuna, drained

¼ tsp Garlic Powder

⅓ cup Sugar-Free Mayo

1 tbsp. Onion Flakes

Preparation:

1. Combine the seasonings, mayo, and tuna in a bowl.

2. Cut the pickles in half. Top each half with the tuna mixture.

3. Place in the fridge for about 30 minutes before serving.

Bacon and Pistachio Liverwurst Truffles

Serves: 8 / Preparation + Cook Time: 45 minutes

Nutritional Info:

Calories 145, Net Carbs 1.5 g, Fat 12 g, Protein 7 g

Ingredients:

8 Bacon Slices, cooked and chopped

8 ounces Liverwurst

¼ cup chopped Pistachios

1 tsp Dijon Mustard

6 ounces Cream Cheese

Preparation:

1. Combine the liverwurst and pistachios in the bowl of your food processor.

2. Pulse until smooth. Whisk the cream cheese and mustard in another bowl.

3. Make 12 balls out of the liverwurst mixture.

4. Make a thin cream cheese layer over. Coat with bacon pieces.

5. Arrange on a plate and refrigerate for 30 minutes.

Mozzarella in Prosciutto Blanket

Serves: 6 / Preparation + Cook Time: 15 minutes

Nutritional Info:

Calories 163, Net Carbs 0.1 g, Fat 12 g, Protein 13 g

Ingredients:

6 thin Prosciutto Slices

18 Basil Leaves

18 Mozzarella Cilliegine (about 8 ½ ounces in total)

Preparation:

1. Cut the prosciutto slices into three strips.

2. Place basil leaves at the end of each strip.

3. Top with mozzarella.

4. Wrap the mozzarella in prosciutto.

5. Secure with toothpicks.

6. Enjoy!

Caprese Turkey Meatballs

Serves: 4 / Preparation + Cook Time: 15 minutes

Nutritional Info:

Calories 310, Net Carbs 2 g, Fat 26 g, Protein 22 g

Ingredients:

1 pound ground Turkey

2 tbsp. chopped sun dried Tomatoes

2 tbsp. chopped Basil

½ tsp garlic Powder

1 Egg

½ tsp Salt

¼ cup Almond Flour

2 tbsp. Olive Oil

½ cup shredded Mozzarella

¼ tsp Pepper

Preparation:

1. Place everything except the oil in a bowl.
2. Mix with your hands until combined.
3. Form 16 meatballs out of the mixture.
4. Heat the olive oil in a skillet over medium heat.
5. Cook the meatballs for about 3 minutes per each side.
6. Serve as desired and enjoy!

Citrus Chicken Wings

Serves: 4 / Preparation + Cook Time: 30 minutes

Nutritional Info:

Calories 365, Net Carbs 4 g, Fat 25 g, Protein 21 g

Ingredients:

1 cup Omission Ipa

Pinch of Garlic Powder

1 tsp Grapefruit Zest

3 tbsp. Lemon Juice

½ tsp ground Coriander

1 tbsp. Fish Sauce

2 tbsp. Butter

¼ tsp Xanthan Gum

3 tbsp. Swerve Sweetener

20 Wing Pieces

Salt and Pepper, to taste

Preparation:

1. Combine lemon juice and zest, fish sauce, coriander, omission ipa, sweetener, and garlic powder in a saucepan.

2. Bring to a boil, cover, lower the heat, and let simmer for 10 minutes.

3. Stir in the butter and xanthan gum. Set aside.

4. Season the wings with some salt and pepper.

5. Preheat the grill and cook for 5 minutes per side.

6. Serve topped with the sauce.

Chicken in Peanut Sauce

Serves: 6 / Preparation + Cook Time: 1 hour and 50 minutes

Nutritional Info:

Calories 492, Net Carbs 3 g, Fat 36 g, Protein 35 g

Ingredients:

1 tbsp. wheat-free Soy Sauce

1 tbsp. sugar-free Fish Sauce

1 tbsp. Lime Juice

1 tsp Coriander

1 tsp minced Garlic

1 tsp minced Ginger

1 tbsp. Olive Oil

1 tbsp. Rice Wine Vinegar

1 tsp Cayenne Pepper

1 tsp Erythritol

6 Chicken Thighs

Sauce:

½ cup Peanut Butter

1 tsp minced Garlic

1 tbsp. Lime Juice

2 tbsp. Water

1 tsp minced Ginger

1 tbsp. chopped Jalapeno

2 tbsp. Rice Wine Vinegar

2 tbsp. Erythritol

1 tbsp. Fish Sauce

Preparation:

1. Combine all of the chicken ingredients in a large Ziploc bag.
2. Seal the bag and shake to combine. Refrigerate for about 1 hour.
3. Remove from fridge about 15 minutes before cooking.
4. Preheat the grill to medium and grill the chicken for about 7 minutes per side.
5. Meanwhile, whisk together all of the sauce ingredients in a mixing bowl.
6. Serve the chicken drizzled with peanut sauce.

Spicy Chicken Skewers

Serves: 6 / Preparation + Cook Time: 1 hour and 20 minutes

Nutritional Info:

Calories 198, Net Carbs 1 g, Fat 35 g, Protein 35 g

Ingredients:

2 pounds Chicken Breasts, cut into cubes
1 tsp Sesame Oil
1 cup Red Bell Pepper pieces
1 tbsp. Olive Oil
2 tbsp. Five Spice Powder
2 tbsp. granulated Sweetener
1 tbsp. Fish Sauce

Preparation:

1. Combine the sauces and seasonings in a bowl. Add the chicken, and let marinate for 1 hour in the fridge.
2. Preheat the grill. Take 12 skewers and thread the chicken and bell peppers.
3. Grill for about 3 minutes per side.

Spinach and Cheese Stuffed Chicken Breast

Serves: 4 / Preparation + Cook Time: 50 minutes

Nutritional Info:

Calories 491, Net Carbs 3.5 g, Fat 36 g, Protein 38 g

Ingredients:

4 Chicken Breasts, boneless and skinless
½ cup Mozzarella Cheese
⅓ cup Parmesan Cheese
6 ounces Cream Cheese
2 cups Spinach, chopped
Pinch of Nutmeg
½ tsp minced Garlic

Breading:

2 Eggs
⅓ cup Almond Flour
2 tbsp. Olive Oil
½ tsp Parsley
⅓ cup Parmesan Cheese
Pinch of Onion Powder

Preparation:

1. Pound the chicken until it doubles in size. Mix the cream cheese, spinach, mozzarella, nutmeg, salt, pepper, and parmesan in a bowl.

2. Divide the mixture between the chicken breasts and spread it out evenly.

3. Wrap the chicken in a plastic wrap. Refrigerate for 15 minutes.

4. Heat the oil in a pan and preheat the oven to 370 degrees.

5. Beat the eggs and combine all of the other breading ingredients in a bowl.

6. Dip the chicken in egg first, then in the breading mixture.

7. Cook in the pan until browned. Place on a lined baking sheet and bake for 20 minutes.

Simple Dijon Chicken Thighs

Serves: 4 / Preparation + Cook Time: 30 minutes

Nutritional Info:

Calories 528, Net Carbs 4 g, Fat 42 g, Protein 33 g

Ingredients:

½ cup Chicken Stock

1 tbsp. Olive Oil

½ cup chopped Onion

4 Chicken Thighs

¼ cup Heavy Cream

2 tbsp. Dijon Mustard

1 tsp Thyme

1 tsp Garlic Powder

Preparation:

1. Heat the olive oil in a pan. Cook the chicken for about 4 minutes per side. Set aside. Sauté the onions in the same pan for 3 minutes, add the stock, and simmer for 5 minutes.

2. Stir in mustard and heavy cream, along with thyme and garlic powder.

3. Pour the sauce over the chicken and serve.

Chicken and Mushrooms in a Skillet

Serves: 6 / Preparation + Cook Time: 35 minutes

Nutritional Info:

Calories 447, Net Carbs 1 g, Fat 37 g, Protein 31 g

Ingredients:

2 cups sliced Mushrooms

½ tsp Onion Powder

½ tsp Garlic Powder

¼ cup Butter

½ cup Water

1 tsp Dijon Mustard

1 tbsp. Tarragon, chopped

4 Chicken Thighs

Salt and pepper, to taste

Preparation:

1. Season the thighs with salt, pepper, garlic, and onion powder.
2. Melt some of the butter in a skillet, and cook the chicken until browned. Set aside.
3. Melt the remaining butter and cook the mushrooms for about 5 minutes.
4. Stir in Dijon Mustard and water.
5. Return the chicken to the skillet.
6. Season to taste with season and pepper.
7. Reduce the heat and cover, and let simmer for 15 minutes.
8. Stir in tarragon.

Turkey Bolognese Veggie Pasta

Serves: 6 / Preparation + Cook Time: 30 minutes

Nutritional Info (not including the veggie pasta):

Calories 273, Net Carbs 3.8 Fat 16 g, Protein 19 g

Ingredients:

2 cups sliced Mushrooms

2 tsp Oil

1 pound ground Turkey

3 tbsp. Pesto Sauce

1 cup diced Onion

2 cups sliced Zucchini

6 cups Veggie Pasta (spiralized)

Fresh basil leaves, to serve

Preparation:

1. Heat the oil in a skillet over medium heat.
2. Add turkey and cook until browned. Transfer to a plate.
3. Add onions to the skillet, and cook until translucent, about 3 minutes.
4. Add zucchini and mushrooms and cook for 7 more minutes.
5. Return the turkey to the skillet. Stir in the pesto sauce.
6. Cover the pan, lower the heat, and simmer for 5 minutes.
7. Serve immediately topped with fresh basil leaves.

Cucumber Salsa Topped Turkey Patties

Serves: 4 / Preparation + Cook Time: 30 minutes

Nutritional Info:

Calories 475, Net Carbs 5 g, Fat 38 g, Protein 26 g

Ingredients:

2 Spring Onions, thinly sliced

1 pound ground Turkey

1 Egg

2 Garlic Cloves, minced

1 tbsp. chopped Herbs

1 small Chili Pepper, deseeded and diced

2 tbsp. Ghee

Cucumber Salsa:

1 tbsp. Apple Cider Vinegar

1 tbsp. chopped Dill

1 Garlic Clove, minced

2 Cucumbers, grated

1 cup Sour Cream

1 Jalapeno Pepper, minced

2 tbsp. Olive Oil

Preparation:

1. Place all of the turkey ingredients, except the ghee, in a bowl. Mix to combine.

2. Make patties out of the mixture. Melt the ghee in a skillet over medium heat.

3. Cook the patties for about 3 minutes per side. Place all of the salsa ingredients in a bowl and mix to combine.

4. Serve the patties topped with salsa.

Hasselback Chicken

Serves: 6 / Preparation + Cook Time: 45 minutes

Nutritional Info:

Calories 338, Net Carbs 2.5 g, Fat 28 g, Protein 37 g

Ingredients:

4 ounces Cream Cheese

3 ounces Mozzarella Slices

10 ounces Spinach

⅓ cup shredded Mozzarella

1 tbsp. Olive Oil

⅔ cup Tomato Basil Sauce

3 Whole Chicken Breasts

Preparation:

1. Preheat your oven to 400 degrees F.

2. Combine the cream cheese, shredded mozzarella, and spinach in the microwave, until the cheese melts.

3. Cut the chicken with the knife a couple of times horizontally.

4. Stuff with the filling.

5. Brush the top with olive oil.

6. Place on a lined baking dish and in the oven. Bake for 25 minutes.

7. Pour the sauce over and top with mozzarella.

8. Return to oven and cook for 5 minutes.

Roasted Chicken with Brussel Sprouts

Serves: 8 / Preparation + Cook Time: 120 minutes

Nutritional Info:

Calories 430, Net Carbs 5.1 g, Fat 32 g, Protein 30 g

Ingredients:

5 pound Whole Chicken

1 bunch Oregano

1 bunch Thyme

1 tbsp. Marjoram

1 tbsp. Parsley

1 tbsp. Olive Oil

2 pounds Brussel Sprouts

1 Lemon

4 tbsp. Butter

Preparation:

1. Preheat your oven to 450 degrees F. Stuff the chicken with oregano, thyme, and lemon. Make sure the wings are tucked over and behind.

2. Roast for 15 minutes.

3. Reduce the heat to 325 degrees F and cook for 40 minutes.

4. Spread the butter over the chicken and sprinkle parsley and marjoram.

5. Add the Brussel sprouts.

6. Return to oven and bake for 40 more minutes.

7. Let sit for 10 minutes before carving.

Creamy Greens and Chicken in a Skillet

Serves: 4 / Preparation + Cook Time: 20 minutes

Nutritional Info:

Calories 446, Net Carbs 2.6 g, Fat 38 g, Protein 18 g

Ingredients:

1 pound Chicken Thighs

2 tbsp. Coconut Oil

2 tbsp. Coconut Flour

2 carp Dark Leafy Greens

1 tsp Oregano

1 cup Cream

1 cup Chicken Broth

2 tbsp. Butter, melted

Preparation:

1. Melt the coconut oil in a skillet and brown the chicken on all sides. Set aside.

2. Meanwhile, melt the butter and whisk in the flour over medium heat.

3. Whisk in the cream and bring to a boil. Stir in oregano.

4. Add the greens to the skillet and cook until wilted.

5. Pour the sauce over, and cook for a minute.

6. Add the thighs in the skillet and cook for an additional minute.

Crispy Lemon and Thyme Chicken

Serves: 4 / Preparation + Cook Time: 1 hour and 20 minutes

Nutritional Info:

Calories 677, Net Carbs 1 g, Fat 61 g, Protein 28 g

Ingredients:

8 Chicken Thighs

1 tsp Salt

2 tbsp. Lemon Juice

1 tsp Lemon Zest

2 tbsp. Olive Oil

1 tbsp. chopped Thyme

¼ tsp Black Pepper

1 Garlic Cloves, minced

Preparation:

1. Combine all of the ingredients in a bowl.

2. Place in the fridge for one hour.

3. Heat a skillet over medium heat.

4. Add the chicken along with the juices and cook until crispy, about 7 minutes per side.

Red Meat

Cheesy Stuffed Venison Tenderloin

Serves: 8 / Preparation + Cook Time: 30 minutes

Nutritional Info:

Calories 194, Net Carbs 1.7 g, Fat 20 g, Protein 25 g

Ingredients:

2 pounds Venison Tenderloin

2 Garlic Cloves, minced

2 tbsp. chopped Almonds

½ cup Gorgonzola

½ cup Feta Cheese

1 tsp chopped Onion

½ tsp Sea Salt

Preparation:

1. Preheat your grill to medium.

2. Slice your tenderloin lengthwise to make a pocket for the filling.

3. Combine the rest of the ingredients in a bowl.

4. Stuff the tenderloin with the filling.

5. Shut the meat with skewers.

6. Grill for as long as it takes to reach your desired density.

Canadian Pork Pie

Serves: 8 / Preparation + Cook Time: 1 hour and 40 minutes

Nutritional Info:

Calories 485, Net Carbs 4 g, Fat 41 g, Protein 29 g

Ingredients:

1 Egg

¼ cup Butter

2 cups Almond Flour

¼ tsp xanthan Gum

¼ cup shredded Mozzarella

A Pinch of Salt

Filling:

2 pounds ground Pork

½ cup Water

⅓ cup pureed Onion

¾ tsp Allspice

1 cup cooked and mashed cauliflower

1 tbsp. ground Sage

2 tbsp. Butter

Preparation:

1. Preheat your oven to 350 degrees F.
2. Whisk together all of the crust ingredients in a bowl.
3. Make two balls out of the mixture and refrigerate for 10 minutes.
4. Combine the water, meat, and salt, in a pot over medium heat.

5. Cook for about 15 minutes. Place the meat along with the other ingredients in a bowl. Mix with your hands to combine.

6. Roll out the pie crusts and place one at the bottom of a greased pie pan.

7. Spread the filling over the crust. Top with the other coat.

8. Bake in the oven for 50 minutes then serve.

Salisbury Steak

Serves: 6 / Preparation + Cook Time: 25 minutes

Nutritional Info:

Calories 354, Net Carbs 2.5 g, Fat 28 g, Protein 27 g

Ingredients:

2 pounds Ground Chuck

1 tbsp. Onion Flakes

¾ Almond Flour

¼ cup Beef Broth

1 tbsp. chopped Parsley

1 tbsp. Worcestershire Sauce

Preparation:

1. Preheat your oven to 375 degrees F.

2. Combine all of the ingredients in a bowl.

3. Mix well with your hands and make 6 patties out of the mixture.

4. Arrange on a lined baking sheet.

5. Bake for about 18 minutes.

6. Serve and enjoy!

Braised Sage-Flavored Lamb Chops

Serves: 6 / Preparation + Cook Time: 1 hour and 25 minutes

Nutritional Info:

Calories 397, Net Carbs 4.3 g, Fat 30 g, Protein 16 g

Ingredients:

6 Lamb Chops

1 tbsp. Sage

1 tsp Thyme

1 Onion, sliced

1 cup Water

3 Garlic Cloves, minced

2 tbsp. Olive Oil

½ cup White Wine

Salt and pepper, to taste

Preparation:

1. Heat the olive oil in a pan over medium heat.
2. Add onions and garlic and cook for a few minutes, until soft.
3. Rub the sage and thyme over the lamb chops.
4. Cook the lamb for about 3 minutes per side. Set aside.
5. Pour the white wine and water into the pan, bring the mixture to a boil.
6. Cook until the liquid is reduced by half.
7. Add the chops in the pan, reduce the heat, and let simmer for 1 hour.
8. Taste and adjust the seasonings.
9. Serve warm.

Grilled Lamb Chops with Minty and Lemony Sauce

Serves: 4 / Preparation + Cook Time: 25 minutes

Nutritional Info:

Calories 392, Net Carbs 0 g, Fat 31 g, Protein 29 g

Ingredients:

8 Lamb Chops

2 tbsp. favorite Spice Mix

1 tsp Olive Oil

Sauce:

¼ cup Olive Oil

1 tsp Red Pepper Flakes

2 tbsp. Lemon Juice

2 tbsp. Fresh Mint

3 Garlic Cloves, pressed

2 tbsp. Lemon Zest

¼ cup Parsley

½ tsp Smoked Paprika

Preparation:

1. Rub the lamb with the oil and sprinkle with the seasoning.

2. Preheat the grill to medium.

3. Grill the lamb chops for about 3 minutes per side.

4. Meanwhile, whisk together the sauce ingredients.

5. Serve the lamb chops with the sauce.

Balsamic Meatloaf

Serves: 12 / Preparation + Cook Time: 1 hour and 15 minutes

Nutritional Info:

Calories 264, Net Carbs 6 g, Fat 19 g, Protein 23 g

Ingredients:

3 pounds ground Beef

½ cup chopped Onions

½ cup Almond Flour

2 Garlic Cloves, minced

1 cup sliced Mushrooms

3 Eggs

¼ tsp Pepper

2 tbsp. chopped Parsley

¼ cup chopped bell Peppers

⅓ cup grated Parmesan Cheese

1 tsp Balsamic Vinegar

1 tsp Salt

Glaze:

2 cups Balsamic Vinegar

1 tbsp. Sweetener

2 tbsp. sugar-free Ketchup

Preparation:

1. Combine all of the meatloaf ingredients in a large bowl.

2. Press this mixture into 2 greased loaf pans.

3. Bake at 375 degrees F for about 30 minutes.

4. Meanwhile, make the glaze by combining all of the ingredients in a saucepan over medium heat.

5. Simmer for 20 minutes, until the glaze is thickened.

6. Pour ¼ cup of the glaze over the meatloaf.

7. Save the extra for future use.

8. Put the meatloaf back in the oven and cook for 20 more minutes.

Shitake Butter Steak

Serves: 1 / Preparation + Cook Time: 25 minutes

Nutritional Info:

Calories 370, Net Carbs 3 g, Fat 31 g, Protein 33 g

Ingredients:

6 ounces Ribeye Steak

2 tbsp. Butter

1 tsp Olive Oil

½ cup Shitake Mushrooms, sliced

Salt and ground pepper, to taste

Preparation:

1. Heat the olive oil in a pan over medium heat.

2. Rub the steak with salt and pepper and cook about 4 minutes per side. Set aside.

3. Melt the butter in the pan and cook the shitakes for 4 minutes.

4. Pour the butter and mushrooms over the steak.

Jerk Pork Pot Roast

Serves: 12 / Preparation + Cook Time: 4 hours and 20 minutes

Nutritional Info:

Calories 282, Net Carbs 0 g, Fat 24 g, Protein 23 g

Ingredients:

4 pound Pork Roast

1 tbsp. Olive Oil

¼ cup Jerk Spice Blend

½ cup Beef Stock

Preparation:

1. Rub the pork with olive oil and the spice blend.

2. Heat a dutch oven over medium heat and sear the meat well on all sides.

3. Add the beef broth.

4. Cover the pot, reduce the heat, and let cook for 4 hours.

Golden Pork Chops with Mushrooms

Serves: 6 / Preparation + Cook Time: 1 hour and 15 minutes

Nutritional Info:

Calories 403, Net Carbs 8 g, Fat 32.6 g, Protein 19.4 g

Ingredients:

1 Onion, chopped

2 cans Mushroom Soup

6 Pork Chops

½ cup sliced Mushrooms

Preparation:

1. Preheat the oven to 375 degrees F.
2. Season the pork chops with salt and pepper, and place them in a baking dish. Combine the mushroom soup, mushrooms, and onions, in a bowl.
3. Pour this mixture over the pork chops.
4. Bake for 45 minutes.

Easy Lamb Kebabs

Serves: 4 / Preparation + Cook Time: 20 minutes

Nutritional Info:

Calories 467, Net Carbs 3.2 g, Fat 37 g, Protein 27 g

Ingredients:

1 pound Ground Lamb
¼ tsp Cinnamon
1 Egg
1 grated Onion

Preparation:

1. Place all of the ingredients in a bowl. Mix with your hands to combine well.
2. Divide the meat into 4 pieces
3. Shape all of the meat portions around previously-soaked skewers.
4. Preheat your grill to medium.
5. Grill the kebabs for about 5 minutes per side.
6. Serve and enjoy!

Keto Bolognese Sauce

Serves: 5 / Preparation + Cook Time: 35 minutes

Nutritional Info:

Calories 318, Net Carbs 9 g, Fat 20g, Protein 26 g

Ingredients:

1 pound ground Beef

2 Garlic Cloves

1 Onion, chopped

1 tsp Oregano

1 tsp Sage

1 tsp Marjoram

1 tsp Rosemary

7 ounces canned chopped Tomatoes

1 tbsp. Olive Oil

Preparation:

1. Heat the olive oil in a saucepan over medium heat. Add onions and garlic and cook for 3 minutes until soft, stirring constantly. Do not burn the garlic.

2. Add beef and cook until browned, about 4-5 minutes. Stir in the herbs and tomatoes. Cook for about 15 minutes.

3. Serve with zoodles or other veggie pasta and grated parmesan chesse.

Tip: The sauce is perfect for freezing, so I often make a double batch and freeze what I will not eat right away. Just double all the ingredients.

To Store: Refrigerate for up to 5 days or frozen for up to 3 months (in individual portions). Thaw in the fridge overnight before warming, or you can also thaw and warm it in a covered pot over low heat on the stovetop.

Keto Burgers

Serves: 4 / Preparation + Cook Time: 15 minutes

Nutritional Info:

Calories 664, Net Carbs 7.9 g, Fat 55 g, Protein 39 g

Ingredients:

1 pound ground Beef

½ tsp Onion Powder

½ tsp Garlic Powder

2 tbsp. Ghee

1 tsp Dijon Mustard

4 Keto Buns

¼ cup Mayonnaise

1 tsp Sriracha

4 strips Bacon

4 tbsp. Slaw

Preparation:

1. Mix together the beef, onion and garlic powder, mustard, salt, and pepper. Create 4 burgers.

2. Melt the ghee in a skillet and cook the burgers for about 3 minutes per side.

3. Remove the meat and add the bacon stripes. Fry until crispy, for a few minutes and drain the excess oil on paper towels.

4. Assemble the burger on a keto bun topped with bacon, mayonnaise, sriracha, and slaw.

Tip: *You can substitute the keto buns with lettuce leaves, for more freshness.*

Seafood

Mediterranean Tilapia

Serves: 4 / Preparation + Cook Time: 30 minutes

Nutritional Info:

Calories 182, Net Carbs 6 g, Fat 15 g, Protein 23 g

Ingredients:

4 Tilapia Fillets
2 Garlic Cloves, minced
2 tsp Oregano
14 ounces diced Tomatoes
1 tbsp. Olive Oil
½ Red Onion, chopped
2 tbsp. Parsley
¼ cup Kalamata Olives

Preparation:

1. Heat the olive oil in a skillet over medium heat and cook the onion for about 3 minutes. Add garlic and oregano and cook for 30 seconds.

2. Stir in tomatoes and bring the mixture to a boil.

3. Reduce the heat and simmer for 5 minutes.

4. Add olives and tilapia.

5. Cook for about 8 minutes.

6. Serve the tilapia with the tomato sauce. Enjoy!

Saucy Salmon in Dill and Tarragon

Serves: 2 / Preparation + Cook Time: 20 minutes

Nutritional Info:

Calories 468.5, Net Carbs 1.5 g, Fat 40 g, Protein 22 g

Ingredients:

2 Salmon Fillets

¾ tsp Tarragon

1 tbsp. Duck Fat

¾ tsp Dill

Sauce:

2 tbsp. Butter

½ tsp Dill

½ tsp Tarragon

¼ cup Heavy Cream

Preparation:

1. Season the salmon with dill and tarragon.
2. Melt the duck fat in a pan over medium heat.
3. Add salmon and cook for about 4 minutes on both sides. Set aside.
4. Melt the butter and add the dill and tarragon.
5. Cook for 30 seconds to infuse the flavors.
6. Whisk in the heavy cream and cook for one more minute.
7. Serve the salmon topped with the sauce.

Nori Shrimp Rolls

Serves: 5 / Preparation + Cook Time: 10 minutes

Nutritional Info:

Calories 130, Net Carbs 1 g, Fat 10 g, Protein 8.7 g

Ingredients:

2 cups cooked and chopped Shrimp

1 tbsp. Sriracha

¼ Cucumber, julienned

5 Hand Roll Nori Sheets

¼ cup Mayonnaise

Preparation:

1. Combine the shrimp, mayo, and sriracha in a bowl.
2. Lay out a single nori sheet on a flat surface and spread about 1/5 of the shrimp mixture.
3. Roll the nori sheet as desired. Repeat with the other ingredients.

Crab Cakes

Serves: 8 / Preparation + Cook Time: 15 minutes

Nutritional Info:

Calories 65, Net Carbs 3.6 g, Fat 5 g, Protein 5.3 g

Ingredients:

2 tbsp. Coconut Oil

1 tbsp. Lemon Juice

1 cup Lump Crab Meat

2 tbsp. Parsley

2 tsp Dijon Mustard

1 Egg, beaten

1 ½ tbsp. Coconut Flour

Preparation:

1. Check to make sure that there are no shells left in the crab meat and place it in a bowl. Add the remaining ingredients, except coconut oil.

2. Mix well to combine. Make 8 crab cakes out of the mixture.

3. Melt the coconut oil in a skillet over medium heat. Add the crab cakes and cook for about 2-3 minutes per side.

Nutty Seabass

Serves: 2 / Preparation + Cook Time: 30 minutes

Nutritional Info:

Calories 467, Net Carbs 2.8 g, Fat 31 g, Protein 40 g

Ingredients:

2 Sea Bass Fillets

2 tbsp. Butter

⅓ cup roasted Hazelnuts

Pinch of Cayenne Pepper

Preparation:

1. Preheat your oven to 425 degrees F. Line a baking dish with waxed paper.

2. Melt the butter and brush it over the fish.

3. In a food processor, combine the rest of the ingredients. Coat the sea bass with the hazelnut mixture.

4. Place in the oven and cook for about 15 minutes.

Battered Shrimp in Creamy Butter Sauce

Serves: 2 / Cook + Preparation + Cook Time: 30 minutes

Nutritional Info:

Calories 560, Net Carbs 4.3 g, Fat 56 g, Protein 18.4 g

Ingredients:

½ ounces grated Parmesan Cheese

1 tbsp. Water

1 Egg, beaten

¼ tsp Curry Powder

2 tsp Almond Flour

12 Shrimps, shelled

3 tbsp. Coconut Oil

Sauce:

2 tbsp. Curry Leaves

2 tbsp. Butter

½ Onion, diced

½ cup Heavy Cream

½ ounce Cheddar

Preparation:

1. Combine all of the dry ingredients for the batter.

2. Melt the coconut oil in a skillet over medium heat. Dip the shrimp in the egg first, and then coat with the dry mixture.

3. Fry until golden and crispy. In another skillet, melt the butter. Add onions and cook for 3 minutes. Add curry leaves and cook for 30 seconds.

4. Stir in heavy cream and cheddar and cook until thickened. Add the shrimp and coat them well.

Blackened Fish Tacos with Slaw

Serves: 4 / Preparation + Cook Time: 20 minutes

Nutritional Info:

Calories 260, Net Carbs 3.5, Fat 20 g, Protein 13.8 g

Ingredients:

1 tbsp. Olive Oil

1 tsp Chili Powder

2 Tilapia Fillets

1 tsp Paprika

4 Keto Tortillas

Slaw:

½ cup Red Cabbage, shredded

1 tbsp. Lemon Juice

1 tsp Apple Cider Vinegar

1 tbsp. Olive Oil

Preparation:

1. Season the tilapia with chili powder and paprika.
2. Heat the olive oil in a skillet over medium heat.
3. Add tilapia and cook until blackened, about 3 minutes per side.
4. Cut into strips.
5. Divide the tilapia between the tortillas.
6. Combine all of the slaw ingredients in a bowl.
7. Divide the slaw between the tortillas.

Chimichurri Shrimp

Serves: 4 / Preparation + Cook Time: 45 minutes

Nutritional Info:

Calories 283, Net Carbs 3.5 g, Fat 20.3 g, Protein 16 g

Ingredients:

1 pound Shrimp, peeled and deveined
2 tbsp. Olive Oil
Juice of 1 Lime

Chimichurri:

½ tsp Salt
¼ cup Olive Oil
2 Garlic Cloves
¼ cup Red Onion, chopped
¼ cup Red Wine Vinegar
½ tsp Pepper
2 cups Parsley
¼ tsp Red Pepper Flakes

Preparation:

1. Place the chimichurri ingredients in the blender. Process until smooth. Set aside.
2. Combine shrimp, olive oil, and lime juice, in a bowl, and let marinate in the fridge for 30 minutes.
3. Preheat your grill to medium. Add shrimp and cook about 2 minutes per side.
4. Serve shrimp drizzled with the sauce.

Baked Salmon with a Pistachio Crust

Serves: 4 / Preparation + Cook Time: 35 minutes

Nutritional Info:

Calories 563, Net Carbs 6 g, Fat 47 g, Protein 34 g

Ingredients:

4 Salmon Fillets

½ tsp Pepper

1 tsp Salt

¼ cup Mayonnaise

½ cup chopped Pistachios

Sauce:

1 chopped Shallot

2 tsp Lemon Zest

1 tbsp. Olive Oil

Pinch of Pepper

1 cup Heavy Cream

Preparation:

1. Preheat the oven to 375 degrees F.
2. Brush the salmon with mayonnaise and season with salt and pepper.
3. Coat with pistachios
4. Place in a lined baking dish and bake for 15 minutes.
5. Meanwhile, heat the olive oil in a saucepan and sauté the shallots for a few minutes. Stir in the rest of the sauce ingredients.
6. Bring the mixture to a boil and cook until thickened.
7. Serve the salmon topped with the sauce.

Pomodoro Zoodles with Sardines

Serves: 2 / Preparation + Cook Time: 10 minutes

Nutritional Info:

Calories 230, Net Carbs 6 g, Fat 31 g, Protein 20 g

Ingredients:

4 cups Zoodles

2 ounces cubed Bacon

4 ounces canned Sardines, chopped

½ cup canned chopped Tomatoes

1 tbsp. Capers

1 tbsp. Parsley

1 tsp minced Garlic

Preparation:

1. Pour some of the sardine oil in a pan. Add garlic and cook for 1 minute.
2. Add the bacon and cook for 2 more minutes.
3. Stir in the tomatoes and let simmer for 5 minutes.
4. Add zoodles and sardines and cook for 3 minutes.

Fried Mac and Cheese

Serves: 7 / Preparation + Cook Time: 45 minutes

Nutritional Info:

Calories 160, Net Carbs 2 g, Fat 12 g, Protein 8.6 g

Ingredients:

1 Cauliflower Head, riced in a food processor

1 ½ cups shredded Cheese

2 tsp Paprika

¾ tsp Rosemary

2 tsp Turmeric

3 Eggs

Olive Oil, for frying

Preparation:

1. Microwave the cauliflower for 5 minutes.

2. Place it in cheesecloth and squeeze the extra juices out.

3. Place the cauliflower in a bowl. Stir in the rest of the ingredients.

4. Heat the oil in a deep pan until it reaches 360 degrees F.

5. Add the 'mac and cheese' and fry until golden and crispy.

6. Drain on paper towels before serving.

7. Enjoy!

Cheesy Bell Pepper Pizza

Serves: 2 / Preparation + Cook Time: 40 minutes

Nutritional Info:

Calories 510, Net Carbs 3.73 g, Fat 39 g, Protein 31 g

Ingredients:

6 ounces Mozzarella

2 tbsp. Cream Cheese

2 tbsp. Parmesan Cheese

1 tsp Oregano

½ cup Almond Flour

2 tbsp. Psyllium Husk

Toppings:

4 ounces grated Cheddar Cheese

¼ cup Marinara Sauce

2/3 Bell Pepper, sliced

1 Tomato, sliced

2 tbsp. chopped Basil

Preparation:

1. Preheat the oven to 400 degrees F.
2. Combine all of the crust ingredients in a large bowl, except the mozzarella.
3. Melt the mozzarella in a microwave. Stir it into the bowl. Mix with your hands to combine. Divide the dough in two. Roll out the two crusts in circles and place on a lined baking sheet. Bake for about 10 minutes.
4. Top with the toppings.
5. Return to the oven and bake for another 10 minutes.

Vegetarian Ketogenic Burgers

Serves: 2 / Preparation + Cook Time: 20 minutes

Nutritional Info:

Calories 637, Net Carbs 8.5 g, Fat 55 g, Protein 23 g

Ingredients:

1 garlic Cloves, minced

2 Portobello Mushrooms

1 tbsp. Coconut Oil, melted

1 tbsp. chopped Basil

1 tbsp. Oregano

2 Eggs, fried

2 Keto Buns

2 tbsp. Mayonnaise

2 Lettuce Leaves

Preparation:

1. Combine the melted coconut oil, garlic, herbs, and salt, in a bowl.
2. Place the mushrooms in the bowl and coat well.
3. Preheat the grill to medium. Grill the mushrooms about 2 minutes per side.
4. Slice the mushrooms and grill them about 2 minutes per side.
5. Cut the keto buns in half.
6. Add the lettuce leaves, then grilled mushrooms, then the eggs, and finally the mayonnaise.
7. Top with the other bun .

White Egg Tex Mex Pizza

Serves: 1 / Preparation + Cook Time: 17 minutes

Nutritional Info:

Calories 591, Net Carbs 2 g, Fat 55 g, Protein 22 g

Ingredients:

2 Large Eggs

1 tbsp. Water

½ Jalapeno, diced

1 ounce Monterey Jack, shredded

1 tbsp. chopped Green Onion

⅛ cup Egg Alfredo Sauce

¼ tsp Cumin

2 tbsp. Olive Oil

Salt and pepper, to taste

Preparation:

1. Preheat the oven to 350 degrees F.
2. Heat the olive oil in a skillet.
3. Whisk the eggs along with water and cumin.
4. Pour the eggs into the skillet. Cook until set.
5. Top with the alfredo sauce and jalapeno.
6. Sprinkle the green onions and cheese over.
7. Place in the oven and bake for 5 minutes.
8. Serve and enjoy.

Fake Mushroom Risotto

Serves: 4 / Preparation + Cook Time: 15 minutes

Nutritional Info:

Calories 264, Net Carbs 8.4 g, Fat 18 g, Protein 11 g

Ingredients:

2 Shallots, diced

3 tbsp. Olive Oil

¼ cup Veggie Broth

⅓ cup Parmesan Cheese

4 tbsp. Butter

3 tbsp. chopped Chives

2 pounds Mushrooms, sliced

4 ½ cups riced Cauliflower

Salt and pepper, to taste

Preparation:

1. Heat two tablespoons of the olive oil in a saucepan.
2. Add the mushrooms and cook over medium heat for about 3 minutes.
3. Remove from the pan and set aside.
4. Heat the remaining oil and cook the shallots for 2 minutes.
5. Stir in the cauliflower and broth, and cook until the liquid is absorbed.
6. Stir in the rest of the ingredients.
7. Taste and adjust the seasonings and serve.

Thyme and Collard Green Waffles

Serves: 4 / Preparation + Cook Time: 45 minutes

Nutritional Info:

Calories 283, Net Carbs 3.5 g, Fat 20.3 g, Protein 16 g

Ingredients:

2 Green Onions

1 tbsp. Olive Oil

2 Eggs

⅓ cup Parmesan Cheese

1 cup Collard Greens

1 cup Mozzarella Cheese

½ Cauliflower Head

1 tsp Garlic Powder

1 tbsp. Sesame Seeds

2 tsp chopped Thyme

Preparation:

1. Place the chopped cauliflower in the food processor and process until rice is formed.

2. Add collard greens, spring onions, and thyme to the food processor. Pulse until smooth. Transfer to a bowl.

3. Stir in the rest of the ingredients and mix to combine.

4. Heat your waffle iron and spread the mixture onto the iron, evenly.

5. Cook following the manufacturer's instructions.

Primavera Spaghetti Squash

Serves: 4 / Preparation + Cook Time: 15 minutes

Nutritional Info:

Calories 139, Net Carbs 6.8 g, Fat 8.2 g, Protein 6.9 g

Ingredients:

1 tbsp. Butter

1 cup Cherry Tomatoes

2 tbsp. Parsley

4 Bacon Slices

¼ cup Parmesan Cheese

3 tbsp. Scallions, chopped

1 cup Sugar Snap Peas

1 tsp Lemon Zest

2 cups cooked Spaghetti Squash

Tip: You can substitute Sugar snap peas with Edamame

Preparation:

1. Melt the butter in a saucepan and cook bacon until crispy.

2. Add the tomatoes and peas, and cook for 5 more minutes.

3. Stir in parsley, zest, and scallions, and remove the pan from heat.

4. Stir in spaghetti and parmesan.

Grilled Cheese the Keto Way

Serves: 1 / Preparation + Cook Time: 15 minutes

Nutritional Info:

Calories 703, Net Carbs 6.14 g, Fat 69 g, Protein 25 g

Ingredients:

2 Eggs

½ tsp Baking Powder

2 tbsp. Butter

2 tbsp. Almond Flour

1 ½ tbsp. Psyllium Husk Powder

2 ounces Cheddar Cheese

Preparation:

1. Whisk together all of the ingredients except 1 tbsp. butter and cheddar.

2. Place in a square oven-proof bowl, and microwave for 90 seconds.

3. Flip the bun over and cut in half. Place the cheddar on one of the bun and top with the other. Melt the remaining butter in a skillet.

4. Add the sandwich and grill until the cheese is melted and the bun is crispy.

Mediterranean Pasta

Serves: 4 / Preparation + Cook Time: 15 minutes

Nutritional Info:

Calories 231, Net Carbs 6.5 g, Fat 20.3 g, Protein 6.5 g

Ingredients:

¼ cup sun-dried Tomatoes

5 garlic Cloves, minced

2 tbsp. Butter

1 cup Spinach

2 Large Zucchinis, spiralized (or peeled with a veggie peeler

¼ cup crumbled Feta

¼ cup Parmesan

10 Kalamata Olives, halved

2 tbsp. Olive Oil

2 tbsp. chopped Parsley

Preparation:

1. Heat the olive oil in a pan over medium heat.

2. Add zoodles, butter, garlic, and spinach. Cook for about 5 minutes. Stir in the olives, tomatoes, and parsley.

3. Continue cooking for another 2 minutes. Stir in the cheeses and serve.

Vegan Olive and Avocado Zoodles

Serves: 4 / Preparation + Cook Time: 15 minutes

Nutritional Info:

Calories 449, Net Carbs 8.4 g, Fat 42 g, Protein 6.3 g

Ingredients:

4 Zucchini, julienned or spiralized

½ cup Pesto

2 Avocados, sliced

1 cup Kalamata Olives, chopped

¼ cup chopped Basil

2 tbsp. Olive Oil

¼ cup chopped Sun-Dried Tomatoes

Preparation:

1. Heat the olive oil in a pan over medium heat. Add zoodles and cook for 4 minutes. Transfer to a plate.

2. Stir in olive oil, pesto, basil, salt, tomatoes, and olives. Top with avocado slices.

Stuffed Portobello Mushrooms

Serves: 2 / Preparation + Cook Time: 30 minutes

Nutritional Info:

Calories 334, Net Carbs 5.5 g, Fat 29 g, Protein 14 g

Ingredients:

4 Portobello Mushrooms

2 tbsp. Olive Oil

2 cups Lettuce

1 cup crumbled Blue Cheese

Preparation:

1. Preheat your oven to 350 degrees F. Remove the stems from the mushrooms. Fill the mushrooms with blue cheese and place on a lined baking sheet. Bake for about 20 minutes.

2. Serve with lettuce drizzled with olive oil.

Desserts

Keto Snickerdoodles

Serves: 4 / Preparation + Cook Time: 25 minutes

Nutritional Info:

Calories 131, Net Carbs 1.5 g, Fat 13 g, Protein 3 g

Ingredients:

2 cups Almond Flour

½ tsp Baking Soda

¾ cup Sweetener

½ cup Butter, softened

Pinch of Salt

Coating:

2 tbsp. Erythritol Sweetener

1 tsp Cinnamon

Preparation:

1. Preheat your oven to 350 degrees F.
2. Combine all of the cookie ingredients in a bowl.
3. Make 16 balls out of the mixture.
4. Flatten them with your hands.
5. Combine the cinnamon and erythritol.
6. Dip the cookies in the cinnamon mixture and arrange them on a lined cookie sheet.
7. Bake for 15 minutes.

Peanut Butter and Chocolate Ice Cream Bars

Serves: 15 / Preparation + Cook Time: 4 hours and 20 minutes

Nutritional Info:

Calories 345 Net Carbs 5 g, Fat 32g, Protein 4 g

Ingredients:

1 cup Heavy Whipping Cream

1 tsp Vanilla Extract

¾ tsp Xanthan Gum

⅔ cup Peanut Butter

1 cup and

1 ½ cups Almond Milk

⅓ tsp Stevia Powder

1 tbsp. Vegetable Glycerin

3 tbsp. Xylitol

Chocolate:

¾ cup Coconut Oil

¼ cup Cocoa Butter Pieces, chopped

2 ounces Unsweetened Chocolate

3 ½ tsp THM Super Sweet Blend

Preparation:

1. Blend all of the ice cream ingredients until smooth. Place in an ice cream mixture (or not if you don't have one) and follow the instructions. Spread the ice cream into a lined pan, and freeze for about 4 hours.

2. Combine all of the ingredients in a microwave-safe bowl and microwave until melted. Slice the ice cream bars. Dip them into the cooled chocolate mixture.

Strawberry Chocolate Mousse

Serves: 4 / Preparation + Cook Time: 30 minutes

Nutritional Info:

Calories 325, Net Carbs 8.1 g, Fat 24.2 g, Protein 11.3 g

Ingredients:

3 eggs

1 cup dark chocolate chips

1 cup heavy cream

1 cup fresh strawberries, sliced

1 vanilla extract

1 tbsp Swerve

Preparation:

1. Melt the chocolate in a microwave-safe bowl in your microwave for a minute on high and let it cool for 10 minutes.
2. Meanwhile, in a medium-sized mixing bowl whip the cream until very soft.
3. Add the eggs, vanilla extract, and swerve and whisk to combine.
4. Fold in the cooled chocolate.
5. Divide the mousse between six glasses.
6. Top with the strawberry slices and chill in the fridge for at least 30 minutes before serving.

Apple Tart

Serves: 8 / Preparation + Cook Time: 65 minutes

Nutritional Info:

Calories 302, Net Carbs 6.7 g, Fat 26 g, Protein 7 g

Ingredients:

6 tbsp. Butter

2 cups Almond Flour

1 tsp Cinnamon

⅓ cup Sweetener

Filling:

2 cups sliced Granny Smith

¼ cup Butter

¼ cup sweetener

½ tsp Cinnamon

½ tsp Lemon Juice

Topping:

¼ tsp Cinnamon

2 tbsp. Sweetener

Tip: Granny Smith apples have just 9.5g of Net Carbs per 100g. Still high for you? Then you can substitute them with Chayote squash, which has the same texture and rich nutrients.

Preparation:

1. Preheat your oven to 375 degrees F.
2. Combine all of the crust ingredients in a bowl.

3. Press this mixture into the bottom of a greased pan.

4. Bake for 5 minutes.

5. Meanwhile, combine the apples and lemon juice in a bowl and let them sit until the crust is ready. Arrange them on top of the crust.

6. Combine the rest of the filling ingredients, and brush this mixture over the apples. Bake for about 30 minutes.

7. Press the apples down with a spatula, return to oven, and bake for 20 more minutes. Combine the cinnamon and sweetener and sprinkle over the tart.

Simple Keto Sherbet

Serves: 1 / Preparation + Cook Time: 3 minutes

Nutritional Info:

Calories 173, Net Carbs 3.7 g, Fat 10 g, Protein 4 g

Ingredients:

¼ tsp Vanilla Extract
1 packet Gelatine, without sugar
1 tbsp. Heavy Whipping Cream
⅓ cup Boiling Water
2 tbsp. mashed Fruit
1 ½ cups crushed Ice
⅓ cup Cold Water

Preparation:

1. Combine the gelatin and boiling water, until dissolved. Transfer to a blender.

2. Add the remaining ingredients. Blend until smooth. Serve immediately cold or freeze.

Raspberry and Coconut Cheesecake

Serves: 12 / Preparation + Cook Time: 4 hours and 50 minutes

Nutritional Info:

Calories 318, Net Carbs 4 g, Fat 31 g, Protein 5 g

Ingredients:

2 Egg Whites

¼ cup Erythritol

3 cups desiccated Coconut

1 tsp Coconut Oil

¼ cup melted Butter

Filling:

3 tbsp. Lemon Juice

6 ounces Raspberries

2 cups Erythritol

1 cup Whipped Cream

Zest of 1 Lemon

3 tbsp. Lemon Juice

24 ounces Cream Cheese

Preparation:

1. Apply the coconut oil to the bottom and sides of a springform pan. Line with parchment paper. Preheat your oven to 350 degrees F.
2. Mix all of the crust ingredients and pour the crust into the pan.
3. Bake for about 25 minutes. Let cool.
4. Meanwhile, beat the cream cheese until soft.
5. Add the lemon juice, zest, and sweetener.

6. In a mixing bowl, beat the heavy cream with an electric mixer.

7. Fold the whipped cream into the cheese cream mixture. Fold in the raspberries gently.

8. Spoon the filling into the baked and cooled crust.

9. Place in the fridge for 4 hours.

Pecan Cookies

Serves: 12 / Preparation + Cook Time: 25 minutes

Nutritional Info:

Calories 101, Net Carbs 0.6 g, Fat 11 g, Protein 1.6 g

Ingredients:

1 Egg
2 cups ground Pecans
¼ cup Sweetener
½ tsp Baking Soda
1 tbsp. Butter
20 Pecan Halves

Preparation:

1. Preheat the oven to 350 degrees F.

2. Mix the ingredients, except the pecan halves, until combined.

3. Make 20 balls out of the mixture and press them with your thumb onto a lined cookie sheet.

4. Top each cookie with a pecan .

5. Bake for about 12 minutes.

Flan with Whipped Cream

Serves: 4 / Preparation + Cook Time: 10 minutes

Nutritional Info:

Calories 343, Net Carbs 2.6 g, Fat 28.6 g, Protein 7.9 g

Ingredients:

1 cup erythritol, for caramel

2 cups almond milk

4 eggs

1 tablespoon vanilla

1 tbsp lemon zest

½ cup erythritol, for custard

2 cups heavy whipping cream

Mint leaves, to serve

Preparation:

1. Heat the erythritol for the caramel in a deep pan.
2. Add 2-3 tablespoons of water, and bring to a boil. Reduce the heat and cook until the caramel turns golden brown.
3. Carefully divide between 4-6 metal tins. Set aside and let them cool.
4. In a bowl, mix the eggs, remaining erythritol, lemon zest, and vanilla.
5. Add the milk and beat again until well combined.
6. Pour the custard into each caramel-lined ramekin and place them into a deep baking tin. Fill one-third of the baking tin with water.
7. Bake at 345 degrees F for 45-50 minutes. Make sure the water doesn't boil. If this happens, add more cold water.
8. Using tongs, take out the ramekins and let them cool for at least 4 hours in the fridge.

9. To serve, take a knife and slowly run around the edges to invert onto dishes.

10. Serve with dollops of whipped cream, scattered with mint leaves.

Chia Pudding with Blackberries

Serves: 2 / Preparation + Cook Time: 10 minutes

Nutritional Info:

Calories 165, Net Carbs 6.8 g, Fat 12.6 g, Protein 7.7 g

Ingredients:

1 cup full-fat natural yogurt

2 tsp Swerve

2 tbsp chia seeds

1 cup fresh blackberries

1 tbsp lemon zest

Mint leaves, to serve

Preparation:

1. Mix together the yogurt and the swerve. Stir in the chia seeds.

2. Reserve 4 blackberries for garnish and mash the remaining blackberries with a fork until pureed. Stir in the yogurt mixture

3. Chill in the fridge for 30 minutes.

4. When cooled, divide the mixture into 2 glasses.

5. Top each with a couple of blackberries and mint leaves.

Saffron and Cardamom Coconut Bars

Serves: 4 / Preparation + Cook Time: 3 hours

Nutritional Info:

Calories 130, Net Carbs 1.4 g, Fat 12 g, Protein 2 g

Ingredients:

3 ½ ounces Ghee

10 Saffron Threads

1 ⅓ cup Coconut Milk

1 ¾ cups shredded coconut

4 tbsp. Sweetener

1 tsp Cardamom Powder

Preparation:

1. Combine the coconut with 1 cup of the coconut milk. In another bowl, mix together the remaining coconut milk with the sweetener and saffron.
2. Let sit for 30 minutes.
3. Heat the ghee in a wok.
4. Add the coconut mixture as well as the saffron mixture, and cook for 5 minutes on low heat, while mixing continuously.
5. Stir in the cardamom and cook for another 5 minutes.
6. Spread the mixture onto a greased baking pan.
7. Freeze for 2 hours.
8. Cut into bars and enjoy!

Berry Clafoutis

Serves: 4 / Preparation + Cook Time: 45 minutes

Nutritional Info:

Calories 198, Net Carbs 4.9 g, Fat 16.5 g, Protein 15 g

Ingredients:

4 Eggs
2 tsp Coconut Oil
2 cups Berries
1 cup Coconut Milk
1 cup Almond Flour
¼ cup Sweetener
½ tsp Vanilla Powder
1 tbsp. Powdered Sweetener
Pinch of Salt

Preparation:

1. Preheat the oven to 350 degrees F.
2. Lace all of the ingredients except the coconut oil, berries, and powdered sweetener, in a blender.
3. Blend until smooth.
4. Gently fold in the berries.
5. Grease a flan dish with the coconut oil.
6. Pour the mixture into the prepared pan.
7. Bake for 35 minutes.
8. Sprinkle with powdered sugar and serve.
9. Enjoy!

Almond and Coconut Bark

Serves: 12 / Preparation + Cook Time: 1 hour and15 minutes

Nutritional Info:

Calories 161, Net Carbs 1.9 g, Fat 15.3 g, Protein 1.9 g

Ingredients:

½ cup Almonds

½ cup Coconut Butter

10 drops Stevia

¼ tsp Salt

½ cup unsweetened Coconut Flakes

4 ounces Dark Chocolate

Preparation:

1. Preheat the oven to 350 degrees.

2. Place the almonds in a baking sheet and toast for 5 minutes.

3. Melt together the butter and chocolate. Stir in stevia.

4. Line a cookie sheet with waxed paper and spread the chocolate evenly.

5. Scatter the almonds on top and sprinkle with salt.

6. Refrigerated for one hour.

Chocolate Mocha Ice Bombs

Serves: 4 / Preparation + Cook Time: 2 hours and 10 minutes

Nutritional Info:

Calories 127, Net Carbs 1.4 g, Fat 13 g, Protein 1.9 g

Ingredients:

½ pound Cream Cheese
4 tbsp. powdered Sweetener
2 ounces Strong Coffee
2 tbsp. Cocoa Powder, unsweetened
1 ounce Cocoa Butter, melted
2 ½ ounces Dark Chocolate, melted

Preparation:

1. Combine cream cheese, sweetener, coffee, and cocoa powder, in a food processor.
2. Roll 2 tbsp. of the mixture and place on a lined tray.
3. Mix the melted cocoa butter and chocolate, and coat the bombs with it.
4. Freeze for 2 hours.

13518165R00061

Made in the USA
Lexington, KY
02 November 2018